Wild Divinity
Lynda Allen

2017

Wild Divinity
By Lynda Allen

Order books from: www.therulesofcreation.com

Copyright © 2017 Lynda Allen
All rights reserved. No part of this book may be reproduced or transmitted in any form or by any means, electronic or mechanical, including photocopying, recording, or by any information storage and retrieval system, without written permission from the author, except for brief quotations for purposes of a book review.

Two excerpts from pp. 1-2, 3, from BEAUTY: THE INVISIBLE EMBRACE by JOHN O'DONOHUE. Copyright © 2004 John O'Donohue.
Reprinted by permission of HarperCollins Publishers.

From Divine Beauty by John O'Donohue published by Bantam Press. Reproduced by permission of The Random House Group Ltd. ©2003

Excerpt from poem by Rumi, translated by Coleman Barks.
Used by permission of Coleman Barks.

Printed in the United States.

Interior photographs ©2016 Shell Fischer, https://mindfulvalley.com/
Layout and design by Amy Bayne, FLAR Publishing, fredericksburgwriters.com
Cover photograph ©2017 Lynda Allen

Allen, Lynda.
    Wild Divinity / by Lynda Allen.
    ISBN-13: 978-0-692- 92867-7

    1.   Spiritual Life -- Poetry. I. Title.

Other titles by Lynda Allen

Poetry

Rest in the Knowing
Illumine

Nonfiction

The Rules of Creation

Fiction

Sight to See

Poems

Wild Divinity — 3

Dawn — 5
Light on the Marsh — 6
The River — 7
Defying Gravity — 8
After the Fall — 9
Freedom Song — 11
Remember — 12
Winter Trees — 13
Winter's Palette — 14
Dusk — 15

The Archer — 21

The Whirlwind and the Kiva — 23
From What Remains — 24
Let It Be — 25
Love Letter — 26
Sacrifice — 27
If Everything Can Disappear — 29
Moments of Love — 30
The Ascent — 31

Beyond the Veil — 37

The Shadow Journey — 41
Through the Darkness — 42
At the Feet of the One — 43
Tea Time Meditation — 45
End Measured Mile — 46
One Breath — 47
Awakened Surrender — 48
A Graced Eye — 49
The Archer II — 50
Passing the Chalice — 51
Stretch Marks — 52
I Love You — 53

Inspirations

It is always fascinating to witness the source of inspiration. This collection is filled with moments of divine inspiration; visits from breathtaking egrets, moments of tenderness in the midst of heart wrenching loss, noticing a sign I've passed dozens of times before and never read. I remember the moment the title poem was born. I had opened John O'Donohue's book *Beauty: The Invisible Embrace* and read a few words of his description of the ocean and its wild divinity, and the words, like the ocean, flowed freely with a beauty and fierceness of their own. John O'Donohue's words and insights also inspired "Defying Gravity," "Awakened Surrender," and "A Graced Eye."

A few of the poems flowed directly from my connection with some of the beautiful people in my life, and those who are no longer in my life, but touched it deeply. "Sacrifice" is in honor of Steve and the bird that helped break my heart open after his passing. "Let it Be" and "Love Letter" are for Kathy and her dear sisters Eleanor and Carolyn. "The Ascent" was a momentary visit with the luminous Ceili, who ascended much too soon, but left a trail of radiant light for us to follow the rest of our days. Finally, "Passing the Chalice," celebrates Christine and the light she shines ever in my life.

Inspiration also comes in the form of friends who offer assistance along the way. This book wouldn't have come into being so beautifully without the exceptional talents and heart of Amy Bayne who lovingly created the layout for the interior and exterior. The magnificent photos that accompany the poems were captured by the gifted Shell Fischer, whose ability to be truly present with the world around her shines through her photographs. Without safe spaces in which to write and invite in inspiration, a writer would be lost. I'm grateful to Susan Carter Morgan for the safe space that she created that allowed so many of these poems to emerge.

for Bill
with wild divinity!

In your light I learn how to love.
In your beauty, how to make poems.

You dance inside my chest
where no-one sees you,

but sometimes I do,
and that sight becomes this art.

- Rumi

Wild Divinity

I want to live with wild Divinity.

I want the secrets of the night
to glow on my moonlit lips.

I want the scent of lavender on a warm breeze
to be my companion for a picnic in the summer meadow.

I want to hold the hand of God,
feeling the beat of Her all-knowing heart in Her fingertips.

I want to immerse myself in the mighty ocean
and celebrate each drop of water within her.

I want to be the perch for the hummingbird,
as he catches his breath for a moment between jousts.

I want to melt with the rocks in the heat of the Earth's belly,
quietly awaiting my chance to soar, flow and transform.

I want to live knowing each moment is one I've never seen before,
nor will ever see again, filled with sweetness and sorrow, light and dark.

I want to be the ray of the sun breaking through the clouds
taking my own breath away with hope, possibility, warmth and light.

I want to be love,
unfettered and free,
tumbling and cartwheeling through the stone gray sky
like an acrobatic snowflake,
only to land gently upon your outstretched tongue,
and melt slowly into you.

Dawn

A sleepy smile greets me at break of day
not awake enough for there to be any veils
between the love within and the love without.
The smile radiates outward
embracing me with its truth.
I am awakened.

Light on the Marsh

The evening was still and quiet, yet teeming with life and deafening with sound.
The white streak of light stood out amid the sunset hues.
The grasses a mixture of oversaturated green and sandy brown,
the sky, shades of pale blue, lavender and dusty rose,
and there she was, brighter than everything around her,
despite her obvious shortage of color.
She stood primly at the marsh's edge without moving.
I paused in my tracks to admire her,
held rapt by her poise and grace.

It wasn't until after she had lifted off
that I realized how much she illuminated everything around her.

By the time I turned upon my tracks to retrace them,
the long fingers of dusk had begun to trail across the tall grasses.
That was the moment when dusk held one finger to the lips of the wandering waters
and whispered, "Shhh,"
and the symphony of sounds began to subside.

When I came again upon her
She had settled atop the ruin of a tree farther from the marsh's edge.
The gathering of nightfall, rather than robbing her of her light,
only made her shine all the more luminescently.
I offered her a slight bow before I continued on,
feeling a twinge of envy at the fallen tree's new found glory.

The River

You can never stand in the same river twice, the wise ones say.

What is the river, truly?
Is she the water she holds?
With her ever present flow, her composition different each moment.
Is she the banks that strive to contain her?
Continuously, bits of them are stripped away and new boundaries formed.
Is she the seemingly immovable rocks she tumbles over?
They are former mountains on their way to becoming pebbles.
Is she simply a winding mirror to show the sky its beauty?
One moment her surface is still and glassy and the next turbulent and dark.
Is she the whole of her journey from spring to delta?
My eyes witness only a tiny stretch of her as I stand in her swirling waters.

Perhaps the lesson then; that I cannot stand in the same river twice because I,
like she,
am not the same person twice.
Each moment different thoughts and emotions flow through me,
each moment I surrender and release bits of myself, pushing my boundaries,
each moment I wear away the immovable within myself,
each moment I reflect the beauty of both the shadow and the light within and above me.
Each conscious moment its own journey from spring to delta.

What then is the river?
I am the river.

Defying Gravity

"In parched terrains new wells are to be discovered."
  John O'Donohue, from *Beauty: The Invisible Embrace*

    Red, dusty, and seemingly parched,
        life yet rises.
    No other description for it, other than
        pale, desert green.
    Hard, cracked surfaces softened by blooms
        of brightest yellow.
    Trees clinging to life upon inhospitable surfaces
        at improbable angles.
    Defying gravity.

    Anchorless, forlorn, and seemingly lost
        life yet rises.
    No other description for it other than
        a soul searching.
    Heart cracked open, ready to soften,
        and to bloom.
    A spirit reawakening upon the hospitable red rocks,
        her improbable angels.
    Defying gravity.

After The Fall

Mighty and graceful she stood.
Not entirely unmovable,
though the wind alone could inspire her to dance.

Year upon year she stood,
year upon year she flourished
and gave forth life.

For time uncounted
her radiance lit that portion of the forest.
Ever she was there reaching skyward,
to drink more of the light.

Only if you knew her
would you have seen the changes that began to appear.
Her posture perhaps not so upright.
A slight change in the texture of her skin.
A diminishing of her strength;
purely physical of course,
for her inner strength had only grown,
it could not be touched by the ravages of time, wind or rain.

Certain enough was that strength,
that she knew from the first
what would happen,
and what it meant.

One glistening morning after a mighty storm,
there was a hole in the forest.
All who lived there felt it.

By the time I happened upon her,
it had been many moons since her fall.
She called to me as I passed
and I sat with her;
still she had the fortitude to hold me.

I placed my hands upon her fading skin
and let my eyes wander along
her once upright and sturdy form.

She had become the home
to many new expressions of life.
She was gradually melting
back into the life giving earth
from which she sprang.

"New life after the fall," she whispered to me.
"There is life, glorious life, after the fall."

Freedom Song

it flutters like a tiny bird upon the edge of the nest
tottering on the brink of eternity
soft, safe nest, or the void?

wings spread, feathers flicker in the breeze
blink and you will miss the leap
made with abandon
and certainty

empty nest sits forlornly among the branches
fragments of shell left behind
like the snake's skin

the song is heard by all who care to listen
freedom sung high and true
joy on the wing
flying free

Remember

Remember, the eagle says,
as he sits serenely in the tree,
at a place where two branches cross.
In stillness, remembering.

Remember, say the leaves
as they fall in an elegant dance,
with gravity as their partner, and wind their music.
In releasing, new life.

Remember, the river calls
as it tumbles past on its journey,
rushing and flowing, always reaching its destination.
In following its course, ease and grace.

Remember, the snake hisses
as he rubs gently against the stone,
sloughing off the skin he no longer needs for the new one beneath.
In chafing, revealing the glimmer within.

Remember, glows the sunflower,
as its whole being slowly tracks
the warmth and light of the sun across the sky.
In waking, facing always the light.

Remember.

Winter Trees

Each leaf now has fallen,
except, of course, for those of the beech.
Some would say they now are barren,
naked.

From my humble perspective
I simply see more of the sky,
and more of their beauty.

Some would say they now are barren,
naked.
I say their true selves are now revealed.

From my humble perspective,
I see their strength, their core.
Each limb reaching in graceful, purposeful elegance
toward the light.

Some would say they now are barren,
naked.
I say they are at their most beautiful
when unveiled.

Winter's Palette

I glance eagerly out the window
to see what colors from winter's palette
the sun has chosen, to paint the trees.
I am not disappointed.

The stark gray of their bark
has been stroked by the
practiced brush of the sun
and is aglow with peach, tinged with pink.

I can see the painted light still drying
on the southeastern side of the trees
and I feel momentary sadness for the side
which the pigment does not reach.

My sadness is short lived
as I recognize that it is the contrast
of the gray against the peach
that makes the colors so brilliant.

It is the shadow together with the light
that creates such beauty to behold.
A secret I suspect Grandfather Sun
already knew.

Dusk

If she could pray, she would,
but the twilight robs her of words.
The mystery is so near, it is all she can do to just breathe
as it takes form —
in the very air in her lungs that animates her being,
in the perfect, intricate design of the willow leaf
twirling in the breeze,
in the angle of the moon as it rises,
slightly more to the south than it was last month.

So tangible is the mystery in the fading light of day,
that it takes up momentary residence beside her,
its hand resting gently upon hers,
a friendship ancient and newborn
moving between them.

To be silent at dusk in the company of mystery,
her living prayer.

The Archer

I'm not sure of the steadiness of the archer's hand, who let me fly.
The trajectory of my life seems circuitous, with no target in sight.
If sin is to miss the mark,
have I then sinned if I don't know the mark I was targeted for?
Can I be blamed for having moved sinuously?

Or must I simply trust the archer's aim?

Perhaps an arrow's purpose can simply be flight.
Perhaps the mark is what lies beyond this life, returning home,
and this whole beautiful existence is simply the flight,
with no bull's-eye intended along the way.

How freeing would it be to know that the target is not here among my days on Earth, but in returning home?

This life then, a flight through the physical, with the goal being to stay aloft,
to ride the winds without being blown far off course,
to hold on to as many of the feathers that make your flight true as you are able,
to keep your head and eyes lifted in order to maintain the arc of your flight.

Let fly my life, let fly my light.

The Whirlwind and the Kiva

"Sanctuary. Sanctuary."
She calls the word out over and over,
as if invoking some ancient rite,
claiming a safe passage.

Then gingerly, one rung at a time, she descends from the whirlwind above,
to the sacred space below.
It is a space where the whirlwind's energy cannot reach her,
a space of stillness and reflection,
where there are no wounds,
only memories of them.

There in that safe, sacred place,
she pulls out the memory of each wound and looks at it differently.
She places each one, great and small,
upon the sacred healing earth before her bare feet.
She stoops and traces her finger along each memory of harm or loss;
some shimmer, some are dark with shadow.

From a pocket she draws a single candle and wooden match.
With gentleness, she strikes the match,
and awakens light in the candle.
She sets the flame amid the wounds and steps back.

The flickering light illuminates her awed smile.

Upon the floor, the scars have come together to form a perfect circle,
a glimmering light at its core.
Rather than a tragic autobiography,
she finds instead, a revealing self-portrait.

She steps within the circle and kneels.
The distant, howling whirlwind takes up the call, "Sanctuary."

From What Remains

The goal, my friend, is not to never have your heart broken,
but is rather, the opposite.
Let it be rent wide open again and again
by expansive, fearless love,
by unbearable pain and sorrow,
by gleeful, exuberant joy,
by vast wells of sadness,
by unending compassion,
by uncontrollable weeping.

Yes, let it be blown asunder
and swept clean by the winds of life

Until the shattered boundaries of your heart
fall as easily away as leaves from the trees in autumn.

Until all that remains of your heart is the Divine.

Live then blissfully from what remains.

Let It Be

Her appearance tells me to let it be.

I don't know how to be
in the face of such loss,
a heart laid so bare.
So I sit with her,
holding her hand in silence.
What good words?
There are none that can reach
into the darkness where she dwells.
The warmth of my hand all she can feel.
Let that be enough for now,
the warmth of a hand in hers,
whatever comfort it may bring,
let it be enough for just this moment.
And then the next.
One breath at a time, hand in hand.
I have no other solace to offer,
beyond a head bent,
a hand strong,
and a heart weeping.
Let it be
enough.

Love Letter

I chose my favorite pen
and a piece of the kind of paper no one uses anymore.
I sat in the comfortable chair by the window and wrote her a letter
her eyes would never read.
For a moment though I felt her,
reading over my shoulder.
Wishful thinking perhaps, yet I know it was her
who nudged me to add that comma.
It annoyed me, just as it always had,
and she laughed, just as she always had.
Saltwater the ink that supplied my pen for the remainder
of my love letter to my sister.

Sacrifice

It was the little bird that broke me.
Until that moment none of it was real,
you weren't gone,
you were just hidden from view,
just playing a cruel game of hide and seek.
Only I had never known you to be cruel.

Until the bird fell
I didn't know it was my heart that had been hidden,
since the moment the phone rang.
Dinner never to be eaten, waited on the table.
Gone? Gone where?

A cry of anguish
that could not be silenced,
leapt from my lips
to the ears of angels,
who now rejoiced in your company.

Emptiness worn like a shroud,
heavy upon my shoulders.
I existed.
Details, others to support,
another's husband,
another's son,
another's brother,
another's father.
Choosing to forget,
that you were my friend.

I buried myself
as much as they buried you.

But that bird,
that bird broke my heart.

The church was empty,
I felt safe, finally, in the silence of that holy place.
With everyone gone,
I could breathe for a moment.

Then I looked up,
a tiny bird fluttered in the rafters
and for a moment hope fluttered.

Maybe it was the hope that startled it.
There was no easy way out;
feather met brick,
and in slow motion it fell
and didn't move again.

I learned there is a tiny sound
when a heart shatters.
You have to listen closely to hear it.

Sorrow washed over what was left,
until I was adrift in it,
watching the fragments float away.

The saltwater of my tears the only thing
that could have begun the healing.

Did the bird know?
His life for the return of mine?
I have been aware of his sacrifice
ever since.

To his credit,
in time I remembered the wholeness
of my unbreakable heart.

Though I admit that there are still moments
when I wish that if only,
like a child,
I could call, "Olly olly all come free,"
and you would appear
laughing
from behind a tree
where a tiny bird is perched.

If Everything Can Disappear

If everything can disappear in a moment, in the blink of an eye, without knowing it's coming, without saying goodbye, without warning, without. Then what is there to hold on to? If I hold you tightly enough can I keep you here, eternally, not going without goodbye, but together always?

If everything can disappear without explanation, without rhyme or reason, then how do I reason, how do I make sense of it, of anything? Why cling to life or you or anyone, if it can disappear as if it never existed, as if you never existed, leaving only the wispy threads of memory?

If everything can disappear then clinging, grasping serves no purpose, you can only hold water in your hands for so long before it drips away. Yet, as I hold the water I can feel its coolness on my palms, I can touch my lips to it and drink, I can see my own reflection on its smooth surface.

If everything can disappear first it must appear, appear in all its glory, in all its beauty, in all its joy and sorrow, and love and grief.
So I will drink from the waters of life as they pass through my fingers, celebrate them, feel their joy, and grief, and love, and look for my reflection in you.

If everything can disappear.

Moments of Love

You left without a word,
without looking back,
without a farewell.
All of that, perhaps, I could have come to terms with,
eventually.
What I can't live with,
what haunts me and
wakes me from my sleep,
is what else you left without.

You left without knowing you are loved.
You left without feeling love surround you.
Saddest of all,
you left without knowing that you are love.

I have no doubt you know it now.
That is small comfort for me lingering here,
though small comfort is better than none.

Still, I wish you had given me one moment,
even if you still had to go afterward,
just one moment,
to remind you of love,
to show you that you are loved,
to be the mirror to reflect the radiant love within you.

One moment of love before you go,
that's all I would have asked.
In the end that's all we really have to offer,
moments of love.

I could have given you one
to take with you on your journey,
like a tiny Polaroid in your pocket,
if only you had let me.

The Ascent

Come, walk with me a while.
The slope here is gentle.
The gradient will increase ere long,
but for now, walk easily beside me.
The trees move gently by.
Occasionally there is a break between stands of pines,
where we can glimpse how far we've come,
not bothering to check how far we have yet to go.
The ascent requires all our focus.
Each step a journey of its own.
No unnecessary words pass between us.

There will be a time, as the grade increases,
when I will have to ask you to turn aside
so that I may travel on alone,
despite your reluctance.
We both know I must make the last few steps in solitude,
with reverence.
Fear not,
as I break free at last of the company of even the trees,
the view from the peak will be the joyful culmination of the climb.

My view is different,
yet still I am able to see you from here.
The steps we took side by side
seen from here as a golden thread in the tapestry of time,
hung gracefully upon the walls of heaven,
the great weaver at Her loom.
In Her hand the thread of my life, not cut short,
but trailing out behind Her still,
so much of the story yet to be told.

The slightest of smiles upon Her lips,
Her hands deftly weave my thread into a new portion of the tapestry.
This ascension then, not the end of the story,
but simply the beginning of the next ascent.

Beyond the Veil

Sitting up amongst the trees she watched the shift happen.
First, the wind shifted slightly.
The birds and squirrel in the sweet gum tree took notice,
some took flight.
Next she heard that the sound of the wind through the trees was
different, rattling the leaves from another direction made a
different song.
The air grew slowly colder.
Gradually the fog that she thought had burned off
began to drift in from the water.
Finally, the sun pulled down a veil of a sheer gray,
obscuring its face behind the intricate lace of the fog.

The whole morning changed its demeanor with a shift in the wind.
Her own reflections could not help but follow suit.
Where her eyes were upon the horizon, looking out,
now the wind changed their direction too.
Part of her wanted to follow the birds example and take flight,
but she remained.
Part of her was concerned that her own song had changed and didn't
want to listen,
but she remained.
Part of her wanted to retreat inside to avoid the chill,
but she remained.
Part of her wanted to blow away the veil that the fog brought so
she could see clearly,
but she remained.
The only way to see what remained of herself was to trust the fog to
be only what it was,
a naturally imposed stillness,
a temporary blindness to what is beyond the veil.

So she remained.
She sat within the mist, feeling the damp, cold, air upon her cheek,
with only her willingness, and an intention to try not to flinch at
what she found there.
Fog you know, muffles sounds beyond the fog and seems to
amplify those within it.

It shrouds the view, sometimes so much that you can forget what clarity looks like.
She reminded herself, more than once or twice, that the conditions were temporary and embraced the echoing stillness within the veil.
What she found there was not what she had feared.
I asked her, what do you find there, when you look deep within?
When you sit within the stillness what do you find?
In a choked voice no more than a whisper she told me.

I find a heart without walls, that is simply light and love in shimmering fluid form.
I find peace that is beyond my understanding.
I find joy overflowing.
I find a capacity to love that I am not able to explain with words.
I find God, with a gentle voice and radiant light.
I find the pathways of time stretching out beyond my sight into unknown realms.

I find knowing, a deep knowing that flows directly from all, from the collective One that we are an expression of. A knowing that provides all with all we need, with the answers that are unanswerable, and that have no need of answers.

I find light and song, sounds that I have not heard upon the earth, and yet that I carry in my heart every moment. Songs without words or music, and yet they are clearly songs. I hear my own voice within the harmony of the song.

I find laughter and tears and realize they are my own. The tears that I have cried for all are here, they float now like droplets of starlight amid the cosmos. The joy that has spilled over in laughter is here too. It bounces like a pinball off the stars, making the universe echo with laughter. I see all that I have felt and cried and screamed and sang and laughed, all here turned into light, the light that helps illuminate the universe.

I see that there are no boundaries, there are no edges, that I naturally flow into all and all flows into and through me. I see that we don't exist separately, but as one fluid expression of love. That even if love becomes stagnant in the human form, when we believe that our artificial boundaries can truly separate us, eventually love will flow, like water does, beyond any boundary or wall, and rejoin the flow.

From here I can see within myself all of this. I can see the radiance that I am. I can see with eyes of compassion and love the path I have walked, the human doubts that have held me in a belief of limitation. I can see my radiant self as part of the one radiance, touching all in each moment, and I am overflowing with joy at the sight.

From here I can see beyond the veil.

The Shadow Journey

The moon's shadow journey,
little by little, step by step,
eclipsing the light.
How can a moon so new, dim a star so bright?
They warn that the moon will blot out the sun.
Yet my eyes see darkness
surrounded by radiant light.
A light so intense
that it cannot be looked upon with the naked eye.
A halo of light
crowning an emerging spring,
and embracing the darkness.

The light reemerges as the shadow journey passes.

Perhaps we are merely in the shadow part of our journey.
Passing between ourselves and the light
and so casting the Earth into temporary darkness.
Yet at that singular moment
when the light seems completely eclipsed,
emerges a light, blindingly bright,
too brilliant for our gaze,
too luminous
to see the work of the light.

If we will but continue on our arc,
the shadow will pass
moment by moment, step by step,
and the light reemerge,
gentle enough for us to look again upon its beauty,
and to bask again in its warmth.

The light reemerges as the shadow journey passes.

Through the Darkness

The stone thrown from the child's hand
skips across the surface,
once, twice, three times,
then descends swiftly, but gently,
making a path through the still water
and stirring up the mud
at the bottom of the pond.

In the darkness it sits,
below the surface,
where it is cold and no sunlight reaches,
where knowing is muted,
where the darkness of the mud cannot be pierced,
nor the murkiness of the water.
Fearful, remaining still,
not knowing that the water
will again become tranquil,
and the mud will settle.

In the light,
upon the surface,
where it is warm and bathed in sunlight,
the lotus sits.
The light it holds within
a beacon easily seen, if looked for.
A strong stem,
reaches deep down from the core,
to the depths of the darkness,
beside the small stone,
into the blinding mud.

A connection through the darkness
which carries nourishment,
which provides the growth
which creates the lotus,
which shines so bright.

At the Feet of the One

There is no place you need go,
No mountain you need climb,
No cave within which you need sit,
No master you need seek.

You need only be awake in each moment.

Look at the delicate beauty of a flower petal,
Drink in its color, inhale its scent, feel its silken touch upon your skin,
And you are sitting at the feet of the One.

Watch the flight of a bird,
See each feather and quill constructed for flight, able to catch and ride the wind with ease,
And you are sitting at the feet of the One.

Feel the warmth and fire of the sun,
Know that light upon your skin brings life to every living thing upon this Earth, simply by shining,
And you are sitting at the feet of the One.

Listen to the sound of the river flow by,
Hear its voice, gentle or raging, speak of the flow of life and the natural cycle of transformation it brings,
And you are sitting at the feet of the One.

Be in the presence of a child,
Look into their eyes brimming with joy and wonder,
experience a moment of painful, unbridled laughter,
And you are sitting at the feet of the One.

Feel, without attempt to lessen it, your grief,
Allow the gaping hole you feel within your being
to expand until you can fall through it, let the deep,
anguished cry of your spirit be heard,
And you are sitting at the feet of the One.

Love without ceasing your beloved,
Trust that there are no boundaries or limits you need put upon your love, share without fear, the depths of your being for another to see,
And you are sitting at the feet of the One.

Let your spirit be alive in each moment,
And you are sitting at the feet of the One.

Tea Time Meditation

The table is set.
Steam rises from the silver pot in the center of the table.
The cups rest neatly upon their saucers,
the spoons waiting patiently beside them.
A petite pitcher of milk awaits pouring,
and a bowl of sugar sits with its lid jauntily atop.
The linen napkins are crisp and simple;
frilly is not called for here.

She greets each graciously as they begin to arrive
and choose their seats.
Impatience is, of course, the first to arrive,
fingers drumming the table as soon as she is seated.
Envy wanders in, casting furtive glances around the room,
and choosing a seat far from Impatience.
The one with a mouth like a sailor strides right in without hesitation,
choosing the seat beside Impatience,
and whispers things to her in language I shan't repeat.
It does not surprise her when Self-Doubt arrives
and quietly takes the seat nearest her.
Finally, Competition arrives,
the brim of a red baseball cap pulled down low over his eyes.

She knows without knowing how that he is the last to arrive,
leaving the seats for Self-Righteousness and Fear of Failure vacant.
She notes their absence and her own progress with a smile,
as she pours the steaming tea for her remaining demons.

End Measured Mile

Three words on a sign I had passed dozens of times,
but never seen before —
End Measured Mile.
Not only words,
not a statement,
a command,
one that my whole being felt.

In that moment a shift.
Just like that.
One moment everything was the same,
then three words seen in passing,
and nothing was the same.
Every cell rearranged.

End. Measured. Mile.

Every single mile I had measured to that point,
every comparison made,
every place where I told myself I fell short of the mark,
every one,
fell away.

End.
Begin.

What a relief, life without an odometer.
Nothing but open road.
A journey not to be measured,
but walked, run, danced, lived
with sorrow and joy immeasurable.

With each step unique,
what then to compare it to?

Unknowable distances yet to cover,
this moment, alone in the woods, the only one that matters.
Until the next.

To end again where I began,
the only measure.

One Breath

She lies still
utterly exposed, like the shore as the wave recedes,
sparkling and teeming with life.
The whisper of the water rushing away over pebbles,
like the whisper of God's voice calling.
That is what she hears now,
in the vulnerable stillness,
the tender murmur of God's voice.
And as the sand draws a deep, gasping breath
once the water has trailed its fingers across its surface,
rushing to carry its secrets to the depths,
so too does she draw a long, gasping breath
as if being revealed in the light for the first time.

Each time she stands naked in the presence of God
is as the first time.

She hardly dares to draw another breath for fear of disturbing the beauty,
or worse yet for fear of being discovered and banished for lack of worthiness.
As if the mighty ocean judges each drop of water that makes it up,
or each grain of sand it touches in its endless ebb and flow.

So she imagines herself floating effortlessly upon the ocean's surface,
buoyed by the gently rolling waves.
She stops holding her breath and simply lets herself drift on the currents of Spirit's motion.
She can feel the tug of the bright light of the distant moon
and moves easily in its direction.
Soon she no longer hears the sighing and whispering of God,
instead only the sounds of steady breathing.
Only the sound of God breathing her.
One ocean.
One breath.
One. Being.

Awakened Surrender

"We live between the act of awakening and the act of surrender."
"Awakening and surrender: they frame each day and each life; between them the journey where anything can happen, the beauty, the frailty."
    John O'Donohue from *Beauty: The Invisible Embrace*

    Awakening and surrender
    the bookends of this human life he says.
    Awakening into this life, into this day,
    and surrendering to the next.
    What magic then if I reversed them?
    What if I tiptoed into the dawn and surprised it with surrender?
    Surrendering my will to the wonder of a new day filled with possibilities beyond my imagining.
    Surrendering to each breath without expectation, knowing the miracle in each moment as it unfolds.

    What then if I laid myself down at the end of my wonder filled day or life with a sense of awakening?
    What unknown wonders would visit me in my awakened dreams?
    What friends past, present, and future would I meet along the pathways of an awakened unknown?

    What if I surrender to this moment and awaken to the next?
    A never ending cycle, gently moving the energy of my existence like the waves breaking upon the shore.
    I surrender to the shore as I wash up upon it, and awaken as I drift gently back into the whole.

    I think he would approve.
    I will ask him when next we meet,
    in the bliss of awakened surrender.

A Graced Eye

To look upon the world
with John O'Donohue's graced eye.
To see the hidden beauty
in everything.
Surely this is the greatest gift I can give,
the most lasting legacy I can leave.

To look upon you
with a graced eye.
To see the beauty
not just in your smile,
or the tilt of your head,
but in the lovely patterns
created by the contrast
of shadow and light within you.

To find beauty in the lilt of your voice,
or the way your heart sifts through
your thoughts for grains of truth.

To see with a graced eye
your actions and choices,
as part of the mysteriously beautiful pathway
on your journey of remembering.

To find the hidden beauty in each moment spent together,
my birthright and my bequest.

The Archer II

An archer stands,
arrow home, ready to fly.
Slow steady breaths
to ensure a smooth and accurate flight.
Hand anchored beside the mouth.

The target beyond the reach of her vision,
yet her aim is true,
for she does not sight it with her eyes,
but with her heart.

The eagle takes flight.
A single white feather drifts slowly back to earth.

A bird's eye view reveals
archers the world over,
arrows home, ready to fly
from millions of hearts.

Archers of love
take aim.

Passing the Chalice

I was witness when you raised the chalice to your lips
and drank deeply of the light.
I watched as the light settled into every part of you,
like it was returning home.
A welcome found within you,
an open heart, ready for the light.
The flood of radiance warming you,
illuminating you,
until you were lit from within.

Only by that light did I truly see.

In the chalice was a spark
that simply fed the light that lived already within you.
A moment of reigniting a mighty fire
with light enough for others to see by
so that you in turn
became the chalice
for others to drink from
to kindle the light within,
to add to the glow
that shines ever on.

Stretch Marks

It must be malleable;
that has to come first.
It will not be able to encompass it
if it will not stretch.

As with the womb, it can be a gradual process.
Over time, what lies within will grow and expand,
stretching its boundaries to allow for the growth.

Sometimes the stretching is gentle.
Other times it feels like an unbearable pressure,
carrying another being within you.

If the boundaries are brittle
they will surely shatter
when exposed to such pressure.

Of course there are moments of unbearable loss or pain,
when shattered is the only suitable description.
There are also moments of love so expansive,
that the walls feel stretched well beyond their capacity.

Like when the babe comes forth fresh and new,
and is first laid in the mother's waiting arms,
a moment of recognition and connection so profound,
the heart easily overflows its bounds.

Let the world then,
with all its loss and suffering,
with all its joy and love,
with all its fear and hatred,
with all its kindness and grace,
be the babe within the womb of your heart.

Allow it to be malleable and stretch,
so it is able to expand beyond its boundaries without breaking,
and bring forth the babe into your waiting love,
that each soul will feel the recognition and connection they seek,
within your wide open heart.

I Love You

I love you.
What if, I love you, was all we could say?

What if our tongues were bound by a spell that would only allow us to
speak those three words?
And we had to mean them to be able to speak them.

How many of us would go through life
silently?

How many of us would lose our voices and have to learn to speak all
over again?

What would our days be like if all we heard was, I love you,
and in hearing those words, we knew the sentiment was true?

I love you.

www.ingramcontent.com/pod-product-compliance
Lightning Source LLC
Chambersburg PA
CBHW042052290426
44110CB00001B/33